AI Capability Building

A Modern Data and Analytics Function

By

Majid Latif Jr., PhD

Majid Latif Jr., PhD

This book is designed to provide information and motivation to our readers. It is sold with the understanding that the publisher and author are not engaged to render any type of psychological, legal, or professional advice. The information contained herein is the author's opinion and experience and should be used at the reader's discretion.

Written by Majid Latif Jr., Ph.D.
Published by Bluebonnet Axiom Group, LLC
Houston, Texas

ISBN: 979-8-9957147-0-5 (Paperback)
ISBN: 979-8-9957147-1-2 (eBook)

Acknowledgements

To my wife, Jenn, and my daughter, Macy: Thank you for your unwavering support and for the adventures that kept me grounded throughout this journey.

To the team members I've had the privilege to lead: Thank you for the opportunity to mentor you; you are the evidence of these frameworks in action.

To my mentors and managers: Thank you for the coaching and the tough love that shaped my perspective. This work was, and will always be, a team effort.

Table of Contents

Preface — 6

Chapter 1: Foundations of Capability Building — 11

  1.1: What is Capability Building? — 12

  1.2: Why the Distinction, and What Does it Mean in Practice? — 14

  1.3: Guiding Principles for Building Functional Capabilities — 16

  1.4: Ultimate Outcomes and Business Value — 18

Chapter 2: Designing the Capability — 22

  2.1: Organizational Design 101: The 5-Step Blueprint — 23

  2.2: The Path to Commercializing Data and AI Engines — 25

  2.3: Selecting an Appropriate Data and Analytics Capability — 28

Chapter 3: Cultivating a Team — 31

  3.1: Architecting the Team — 32

  3.2: Staffing the Team from The Ground Up — 37

  3.3: Scaling the Team while Delivering Value — 42

  3.4: Evolving the Team's Charter and Design — 49

Chapter 4: Sustaining a High Performance Team — 53

  4.1 Competency, Skills, and Calibration Matrix — 54

  4.2 Personal Development Culture and Routines — 62

  4.3: Invest in Your Managers — 67

Chapter 5: Evolving the Capability with Business Needs — 72

  5.1 Work Intake and Roadmaps — 73

  5.2: Use case Lifecycle — 77

  5.3: Extending the Use Case Life Cycle for Generative AI — 82

Outro — 89

Appendix: Unsolicited Advice 91

 A.1: The Individual Contributor 92

 A.2: The First Line Manager 94

 A.3: The Intermediate Manager 96

 A.4: The Department Lead 98

 A.5: The Executive Sponsor 99

Bibliography 100

Preface

I have spent several years contemplating a book that captures my professional journey and successes. My goal has been to provide a pragmatic reference guide focused on lessons learned and best practices, rather than a novel. This work intentionally bypasses the mathematical and technical depths of Statistics or Machine Learning, as there is a wealth of existing content, allowing me to hone in on a unique value proposition: sharing my expertise in building functional capabilities through the lens of Data and AI transformation. The title "AI Capability Building" serves as a broad shorthand for a framework relevant across functional Analytics, Operations Research, Data Science, and Advanced Analytics teams. Our objective transcends individual business or mathematical disciplines, focusing instead on achieving sustainable growth via holistic business transformation. To maintain this focus on capability architecture, I have strictly confined the scope to the consumption side of data and technology. I have purposefully excluded in-depth discussions on infrastructure—such as Data Engineering and Warehousing—or the complexities of MLOps. Furthermore, while I acknowledge the critical nature of Data Governance and Privacy, I treat them as necessary prerequisites rather than central topics. Broader Technology foundations, Data Governance, and Product Management may be explored in future books.

The true essence of this Data Driven Business Transformation lies in the seamless integration of production-grade, mathematically-driven insights into the user experience or business processes, sparking the specific actions necessary to drive quantifiable P&L

outcomes. While these concepts are not entirely revolutionary, I aim to provide a pragmatic blueprint for their application to achieve meaningful change. By sharing my personal motivations and strategic approaches, I hope to provide the context you need to adapt these frameworks to your unique organizational environment and realize significant business value.

Inspiration and Motivation

Before exploring the structure, I want to share the driving force behind the experiences that inspired this work. Although I am known for many things, patience is certainly not one of them—a trait my wife suggests is likely genetic. This impatience naturally extends into my professional life. Throughout my career, whenever I faced significant challenges, my mentors would consistently advise me that "it takes time." Unsurprisingly, my response was always to set an incredibly short time box and one up my own expectations.

One of my most significant hurdles was transitioning into a department leader while maintaining my Standard of Excellence amid expanding responsibilities. I achieved success through a combination of formal training, mentorship, 360-degree feedback, and the chance to refine my leadership style alongside exceptional team members. This approach allowed me to effectively double my team size three times every 18 months. I met my own high expectations by: 1) Dedicating time to late-night study of leadership and business theory. 2) Embracing discomfort by failing fast and learning through feedback. 3) Committing to the idea that small, 1% daily improvements add up over time.

Personal Reading List

I offer this list because I am frequently asked how I "figured this out" or how to apply these concepts to specific situations. My answer is consistent: I invest heavily in personal growth through routine reading, a strong mentorship network, and diligent follow-through on feedback.

I maintain a disciplined quarterly reading rotation: the first month focuses on technical skills, the second on managerial and leadership abilities, and the third on business acumen. I select technical topics based on my current projects or those of my mentees, starting with articles and blogs before moving into white papers and open-source repositories. My leadership reading is guided by mentor and peer suggested reading list, while my business acumen study draws from MBA syllabi, consulting firm insights, and MOOC courses. By following this homework schedule regimen, I am equipped to anticipate shifting business needs and serve as an effective strategic advisor for my team and executive sponsors.

Beyond this general rotation, three primary influences shaped my personal leadership philosophy and functional management style: *Extreme Ownership* by Jocko Willink and Leif Babin, *FYI: For Your Improvement* by Michael M. Lombardo, and *The Leadership Pipeline* by Ram Charan, Stephen Drotter, and James Noel. Discovered through mentor feedback, these resources were transformative. *Extreme Ownership* helped me successfully transition to a functional leadership role. *FYI* was invaluable for building a business vernacular—crucial for someone from a STEM-heavy background—and providing a framework for skill assessment.

Finally, *The Leadership Pipeline* was key for me developing the ability to engage and lead org design exercises and gaining alignment with HR and executive sponsors.

How to use the book

The following chapters guide you through the end-to-end journey of building a robust capability. While reading the full text offers the most comprehensive insight, you can also navigate directly to the sections most relevant to your current needs:

- Chapter 1: Foundations of Capability Building. Defines the core objectives and provides a high-level walkthrough of the design, staffing, and cultivation stages.

- Chapter 2: Designing the Capability. Establishes the functional charter and maps the progression from basic reporting to advanced research and innovation.

- Chapter 3: Cultivating a Team. Details the practicalities of organizational design, talent acquisition, and long-term team evolution.

- Chapter 4: Sustaining a High-Performance Team. Focuses on the specific routines and frameworks required to maintain excellence over time.

- Chapter 5: Evolving the Capability with Business Needs. Covers intake, roadmapping, and the product lifecycle, with a focus on making AI integration practical.

- Appendix: Unsolicited Advice. Offers targeted, level-specific mentorship for everyone from individual contributors to executive sponsors.

Chapter 1: Foundations of Capability Building

Welcome to the foundation of Capability Building. This chapter establishes the philosophical and strategic groundwork for the entire playbook. We will move beyond common practices of delivering analytical insights or models, instead focusing on creating a scalable, self-sustaining capability within your organization. We begin by clearly defining Capability Building and its components (Section 1.1), followed by a case study of why this distinction matters in practice when translating outputs into outcomes (Section 1.2). Next, we will introduce nine guiding principles that underpin all successful capability build out (Section 1.3), concluding with a review of ultimate outcomes and quantifiable business value (Section 1.4). We will now start by directly answering the question: What is Capability Building?

1.1: What is Capability Building?

Let's answer the million or even billion dollar question, "What is Capability Building?". *Capability Building* is the explicit mission to design the capability and cultivate a team that can sustain high performance while evolving with changing business needs. I think of Capability Building as a functional roof, like Data and AI, supported by four vertical pillars. True capability is only achieved when all four pillars are established and linked, transforming a static department into a self-reinforcing flywheel that generates increasing momentum and measurable outcomes across multiple business cycles:

- Designing the Capability: Translates the strategic vision into an actionable, commercialized function by articulating the one-liner charter, mapping the organizational design to roles and processes, and selecting the capability archetype for execution.

- Cultivating the Team: The end-to-end talent lifecycle, from architecting the initial organizational structure and defining job families, to strategically staffing, pragmatically scaling the team, and managing its evolution through organizational change and new technology demands.

- Sustaining A High Performance Team: Establishes the routines and management processes—such as talent assessment and development plans—that continuously hone the team's technical and business skills to reliably deliver production-grade output and translate it into measurable business outcomes.

- Evolving the Capability with Business Needs: This is the strategic pillar, ensuring the capability remains relevant by actively planning for and adapting to shifting business priorities, new data sources, and emerging technologies (like Generative AI) across multiple business cycles.

1.2: Why the Distinction, and What Does it Mean in Practice?

To understand why Capability Building matters, we need to look at the difference between an Output and an Outcome. Think of an Output as the actual thing you make or do—like a spreadsheet, a dashboard, or a math model. An Outcome, however, is the real-world result of that work that actually helps the business, like driving revenue growth, increasing margins, or achieving cost savings. Capability Building is all about making sure we can consistently bridge that gap, which is where many new departments' pilot projects fail when they don't deliver the expected outcomes.

Consider a common use case: dashboard rationalization. Company A's revenue doubled over five years, but its dashboard count grew ten-fold. A team was tasked with cutting dashboards by 50% to optimize costs. They identified that 60% of dashboards had low to no utilization and successfully deleted the dashboards with no changes to data or processing pipelines. At face value, the project met its target.

However, this failed to deliver the expected Outcome. The team delivered an Output (deleting low- to no-use dashboards) and not an Outcome. The real Outcome—optimizing operational cost—required identifying the 5% of complex dashboards accounting for 50% of the cost that should have been rationalized through governance for redundancy, which would have resulted in a relative 65% cost savings. Because the team lacked a rigorous framework to translate their Output into business Outcomes, and possibly the required technical and business skills, the resulting reduction was temporary noise rather than a meaningful and measurable business transformation. The processes outlined in the Capability Building framework ensure that we aren't just hiring a team with the correct skills to create dashboards or build models (Output), but creating a permanent organizational ability to build and maintain products that enable and drive business value (Outcome) by integrating the four pillars—Designing the Capability, Cultivating a Team, Sustaining a High Performance Team, and Evolving the Capability with Changing Business Needs—into every initiative.

1.3: Guiding Principles for Building Functional Capabilities

To successfully build the four vertical pillars of Capability Building—Designing the Capability, Cultivating a Team, Sustaining A High Performance Team, and Evolving the Capability with Business Needs—we adhere to nine Guiding Principles (GP). These principles ensure that every framework and process we implement remains pragmatic, scalable, and deeply integrated with the core business mission.

1. "It has to make business sense and value": Every capability requires executive sponsorship and financial backing, justified by customer value, clear ROI and business priorities.

2. "Everyone is a change agent": Empowering every team member to drive transformation ensures the sustainability of the operating model.

3. "Theoretical max potential vs. ability to actualize potential": Prioritize outcomes that are most likely to be achieved over those that are theoretically ideal but practically less feasible.

4. "Aim for scale": Design outputs for future automation and modularity in mind to avoid excessive technical debt.

5. "Invest and empower people": Success is driven by the collective growth of the team; technical experts must eventually outscale themselves by mentoring others.

6. "Don't skip change management": Effective implementation requires empathy, clarity, and empowerment to bridge the gap between Strategy and Execution.

7. "Commercialize your product": Treat technical outputs as "engines" that business owners can easily use to drive, regularly maintained, and available to meet daily needs for incremental value.

8. "Objective vs. Utility function": Use quantitative measures to facilitate informed data driven decision-making and bridge the gap between technical rigor and business needs.

9. "Innovate responsibly": As technology evolves, maintain a commitment to ethical practices and the long-term well-being of team members, end users, and business sponsors.

These principles will serve as critical reference points, reinforced at the conclusion of every major section from Chapter 2 onward to demonstrate their practical application. We will now conclude this chapter by illustrating how these principles guide the achievement of ultimate business outcomes and quantifiable value.

1.4: Ultimate Outcomes and Business Value

Let's tie the 9 guiding principles togethering with a bit of picture perfect story board, the revenue rocket scenarios. Imagine a mid-sized e-commerce company struggling to personalize customer experiences, leading to stagnant sales. The executive team sees a clear opportunity for an analytics team to boost revenue through data-driven personalization.

Here's how the 9 principles guide their journey to a high ROI:

1. "It has to make business sense and value": The executive sponsor champions the analytics team, clearly articulating the business need for personalized customer journeys to unlock millions in incremental revenue. The CFO signs off on the budget after seeing the clear potential for a high ROI from increased sales and customer lifetime value.

2. "Everyone is a change agent": From the new analytics team members to the digital marketing team members, everyone understands they have a role in driving this transformation. They proactively embrace new data-driven insights and processes.

3. "Theoretical max potential vs. ability to actualize potential": Instead of aiming for a perfectly individualized model right away, the team focuses on a "minimum viable personalization" that can be quickly implemented and show initial impact. They prioritize a targeted email campaign that's 50% more effective than current

methods, acknowledging the practical implementation challenges that inform the roadmap for continuous improvements.

4. "Aim for scale": From day one, the team designs their personalization algorithms and data pipelines to be modular and scalable. Their first win with email personalization is built with the underlying architecture to easily expand to website recommendations and app notifications.

5. "Invest and empower people": The company prioritizes investing in its personnel, hiring data science and business analytics practitioners to bridge the technical and marketing divide, and extending investment to training the marketing team to effectively utilize new analytics tools and to make data driven decisions.

6. "Don't skip change management": The analytics and marketing teams collaborate closely. They run pilot programs, gather feedback, and continuously refine the personalization strategies. The marketing team is trained, and regular communication ensures smooth adoption, addressing any resistance with empathy and clarity.

7. "Commercialize your product": The analytics team doesn't just build models; they "productize" their personalization engine. It's integrated directly into the marketing automation platform, making it easy for marketers to deploy targeted campaigns and see the impact.

8. "Objective vs. Utility function": They meticulously track the impact of the personalization engine, using metrics like precision and recall alongside click-through rates, conversion rates, and average order value through experimentation methods like A/B test. They prioritize models that deliver tangible business utility (e.g., increased purchase frequency) over those that are theoretically elegant and minimal conversions.

9. "Innovate responsibly": As they explore more advanced personalization, like leveraging AI, they establish clear guidelines for data privacy and ethical use. They ensure customer data is handled securely and transparently, building trust while driving innovation.

The Reward

The ultimate reward of Capability Building is to move beyond models and insights (Output) and build "Engines" that are directly integrated into business processes to facilitate changes with measurable business outcomes, like Operating Income growth. I am notorious for using the word "engine" because I believe framing it this way clarifies that the underlying model, AI, or logic is just the *output*. The *outcome* is a functional, durable machine, like a car engine, that allows the user (the business sponsor) to drive to the location of their choice. This single term simplifies conversations and creates flexibility for the working team throughout the project.

Now let's get back to how the Revenue Rocket scenario perfectly illustrates the four parts of our core Capability Building definition:

1. "Designing the Capability": The team established the functional blueprint for the "personalization engine" capability, translating the strategic design into integrated, data-driven action within the marketing automation platform.

2. "Cultivate a Team": The scenario shows investment in strategically staffing key roles, training cross-functional partners like marketing, and fostering a successful environment to retain valuable talent.

3. "Sustaining a High Performance Team": The scenario highlights that building a self-sustaining operating model is contingent upon ensuring the team has and continuously cultivates the necessary technical and process skills to reliably deliver the expected, production-grade output over the life of the product.

4. "Evolving the Capability with Business Needs": This addresses the product mindset, emphasizing that the capability must have a clear roadmap and a continuous improvement loop that spans from foundational Analytics to Data Science based models, and ultimately to advanced AI-based personalization. This evolution is achieved in a self-funding manner by leveraging continuously delivered value to fund incremental work.

Now that we have established the foundational 'why' and ultimate value of Capability Building, Chapter 2 will guide us through the initial phase of execution: transforming this conceptual framework into a tangible, organizational design.

Chapter 2: Designing the Capability

In Chapter 1, we established the foundational "why" of Capability Building, defining it as a function supported by four core pillars: Designing the Capability, Cultivating a Team, Sustaining a High Performance Team, and Evolving the Capability with Business Needs. Now, we turn our attention to the initial phase of execution—transforming this conceptual framework into a tangible, organizational design that can deliver measurable outcomes. This chapter focuses on creating the blueprint for your functional capability. We begin with A Crash Course to Org Design 101 (Section 2.1), which outlines a simplified five-step process for mapping a strategic vision to roles and responsibilities. This foundation leads us to define the core mission, synthesized in The Path to Commercializing Analytics Engines (Section 2.2), which provides a one-liner functional charter and its necessary components. We will conclude by discussing the evolutionary path and Selecting an Appropriate Analytics Capability (Section 2.3), detailing the archetypes—Strategic Insights & Reporting, a Model Factory, and Innovation & Research—to ensure your design is correctly calibrated to your organization's maturity and current business needs.

2.1: Organizational Design 101: The 5-Step Blueprint

While numerous formal books have been written on the complexities of Organizational Design, I am sharing a quick, simplified version of my personal mind map—a 5-minute 101—to drive home the core points of our framework. The five steps for my simplified org design process are 1) Functional Charter, 2) Internal and External Processes, 3) Competencies and Skills, 4) Roles and Responsibilities Decomposition, and 5) Working Model. These five steps are solely focused on the design.

The Functional Charter defines the "why" and "what" of the team or capability: the mission, vision, strategic objectives, and scope of the new or redesigned organization/function. Internal and External Processes are the "how" the work gets done once the charter is established, i.e. workflow design, process mapping, and operational procedures. **Competencies and** Skills are the inventory of colleague capabilities required to execute the processes. Next, Roles and Responsibilities define the specific job families and designs—for example, how IC and manager levels are rationalized into a design that is company and market relevant. Finally, the Working Model is the decomposition and assignment of the sub-steps of the internal and external processes across job families and levels.

I want to emphasize why I was so intentional about the order of this five-step blueprint. It's a common mistake to rush into picking "industry-standard roles and responsibilities"—moving Step 4 to be Step 2—especially when inheriting teams. This causes a conflict, like trying to fit a square peg into a round hole, and requires a much larger investment in change management. Data and AI structures vary so much across the Fortune 500 precisely because every company is different. I've found it's much more effective to define your actual processes and required skills first (Steps 2 and 3). Then you can rationalize existing and new roles and responsibilities (Step 4). This sequence is much more effective because it highlights where your processes and roles might clash, allowing you to get things figured out during design instead of having to be reactive during implementation. This is even more important for success when you're working with a tight starting budget.

The preceding steps help you navigate inevitable conflicts, such as when you define a Data Analyst profile that requires a strong technical skill set, but must also possess the basics of process design for adoption to ensure their outputs translate into measurable business outcomes. You must then decide whether to modify the job description to include these cross-functional competencies or forgo the skill set in the team. Given the sensitivity of these decisions—especially those related to existing roles, job architecture, and compensation standards—you need to ensure you have the appropriate level of HR leadership engaged. This entire framework is designed to satisfy GP 1 ("It must make business sense and value") and GP 3 ("Theoretical max potential vs. ability to actualize potential"), ensuring the design is pragmatic and aligned with organizational reality. Having established these foundational steps, we now turn our attention to defining a Functional Charter for a Data and AI function designed to effectively productize and commercialize analytical engines and products.

2.2: The Path to Commercializing Data and AI Engines

I usually synthesize the functional charter of a Data and Analytics function into the following one-liner: "To Productionize, Productize, and Commercialize analytical engines that support business process transformation, digital and data strategy, and measurable financial outcomes."

This charter is built on three essential Core Components that are must-haves for creating business value, complemented by three Force-Multiplying Components that create leverage and opportunities for long-term optimization.

Three Core Components (Must-Haves):

1. Technical Talent and Deployment: Having the technical expertise to build and deploy production-quality analytics engines and data products. The type of engine being built will inform the required analytics talent, and also dictate the necessary data and software engineering support for production deployment.

2. Product Lifecycle Capacity: Establishing capacity to support the analytics engine throughout its product lifecycle instead of as a one-time project. This includes performance monitoring, maintenance support, and a sustained roadmap of incremental features.

3. Commercialization and Governance: The main goal is to empower stakeholders with the knowledge, outputs, and

governance required to leverage and articulate the analytics engine within their day-to-day responsibility as a business process owner.

Three Force-Multiplying Components (Nice-to-Haves):

1. Business Process Transformation: When newly built analytics engines simplify and transform an existing business process, they create secondary benefits in funding unfunded processes, workflow consolidation, and modernizing compliance.

2. Technology Synergy: This component is technological, where modernization and investment synergy create funding opportunities by replatforming, modernizing legacy systems, and elevating the organization's cyber security posture.

3. Portfolio Experimentation and Measurement: Creating individual engine and portfolio-level experimentation and measurement to inform ROI financial insights, which allows for portfolio rationalization and optimization as business priorities evolve.

This functional charter and its six components are based on four of the nine Guiding Principles. These principles keep the team focused on delivering results and real business value. While GP 7 ("Commercialize your product") and GP 4 ("Aim for Scale") serve as the self-evident bedrock for operationalizing engines, GP 1 ("It has to make business sense and value") and GP 8 ("Objective vs. Utility function") represent an attainable progression in maturity. This set of core and force multiplying components creates a way to calibrate current gaps and aspirations that are needed to help select where to start in your analytics journey, as an archetype, and its progression, which we will discuss in Section 2.3.

2.3: Selecting an Appropriate Data and Analytics Capability

Selecting the right Data and Analytics capability is less about choosing a final structure and more about mapping an evolutionary journey, which is why I categorize maturity into three Capability Archetypes. While the implemented design of these archetypes will be unique to a company's industry and existing maturity, they collectively form a clear and necessary path for progression, which requires the corresponding supporting functional dependencies. The three Analytics Capability Archetypes are Strategy Insights & Reporting, Model Factory, and Innovation & Research. The Strategic Insights & Reporting archetype supports business leaders in making process and strategy design decisions. A Model Factory is where models are designed and deployed into core business technology systems. Innovation and Research exist for discovery and prototyping of Next-Gen business solutions.

We can build a classic storyboard for the sequential progression by beginning when a company embarks on a digital, data, or analytics transformation to make data-driven decisions. The natural starting place is building a Strategic Insights & Reporting capability, which requires standardized data access and quality to enable reporting and business analytics models. The outputs are used by a business process owner or leader to inform tactical and strategic decisions. This stage requires strong visualization and some statistical and mathematical knowledge. The end user leveraging Data analytical output can use common sense, business context, and intuition to compensate for less mathematical rigor. Eventually, as demand and potential ROI grow, business leaders support and sponsor extending the capability into a Model Factory archetype. This requires a significant step up in technical skill and rigor. Software engineering practices—like coding standards, code reviews, unit/QA testing, and MLOps—become essential for operating at full-scale in production systems. Since these models run in production and directly trigger business decisions, strong mathematical, statistics, and experimentation knowledge is required for responsible and effective deployment. Finally, once the company sees the consistent yield from the Strategic Insights & Reporting and Model Factory capabilities, freed-up capacity and reinvested funds allows them to expand focus to the Innovation & Research capability to become and maintain an industry-leading Customer Experience and Operational Excellence powerhouse.

I advocate for a tiered development strategy—especially when bootstrapping the build-out without external consultancies. Initially, we anchored the function with Strategic Insights & Reporting, then scaling into a Model Factory, and finally maturing into an Innovation & Research powerhouse. While abundant funding might enable concurrent paths for the first two, I favor this staged evolution because Innovation & Research is most effective when it builds upon established foundations. Without the bedrock of Strategic Insights & Reporting and a Model Factory, advanced research becomes exponentially more difficult to execute and realize an ROI. Consider the adoption curve: users accustomed to traditional analytics or standard Machine Learning models are far more likely to embrace complex, "black-box" engines than those lacking a baseline comfort with data-driven insights. To conclude this discussion, we'll be reinforcing our fundamental Guiding Principles.

By aligning with GP 1 ("It has to make business sense and value") and GP 3 ("Theoretical max potential vs. ability to actualize potential"), an organization can guarantee that advanced technical capabilities are only deployed when the requisite governance and technical maturity exist to yield measurable results. Furthermore, following this progression into a research-oriented archetype empowers the team to Innovate responsibly, GP 9 ("Innovate responsibly"), utilizing a strong foundation of institutional expertise and established protocols to uphold operational excellence and ethical standards as technology advances. In the upcoming chapter, my focus will shift to the simultaneous development of Strategic Insights & Reporting and a Model Factory as the core organizational capability, subsequently using Innovation & Research as a primary case study for the continued evolution of organizational design.

Chapter 3: Cultivating a Team

In Chapter 2, we finalized the blueprints for our Analytics capability, defining the organizational design, functional charter, and capability archetypes. Now, we shift our focus to the next and a critical pillar of Capability Building: Cultivating a Team. A perfect organizational design remains a theoretical exercise until it is brought to life with high-performing talent. This chapter walks through a pragmatic, end-to-end process of building your team. We begin by Architecting the Team (Section 3.1), rationalizing competencies and skills into job families for both Strategic Insights & Reporting and Model Factory archetypes. Next, we cover Staffing the Team from the Ground Up (Section 3.2), detailing the recruiting process and managing the trade-offs of internal versus external talent. We then discuss Scaling the Team while Delivering Value (Section 3.3), focusing on leveraging contractors and process standardization to ensure scalable growth does not halt outcomes. Finally, we address Evolving the Team's Charter and Design (Section 3.4) through case studies on managing organizational change and new technology demands.

.

3.1: Architecting the Team

Let's discuss the process of architecting an organizational design with the goal of building two analytics archetypes: 1) Strategic Insights & Reporting (SIR) and 2) Model Factory (MF). As a reminder, Strategic Insights & Reporting aims to deliver insights to help users make better business decisions, while a Model Factory aims to systematically scale decision-making by directly integrating analytics engines into technology applications. I acknowledge there are grey areas in practice, but for the sake of conversation, we will create a clear dichotomy. These two design decisions complete Steps 1 and 2 of our Simplified Org Design process. Next, we need to discuss Step 3: Competencies and Skills, followed by Step 4: Roles and Responsibility Decomposition, and Step 5: Working Model.

Step 3: Competencies and Skills is where we begin to identify the capabilities needed to accomplish the defined work. I usually categorize competencies and skills into four areas: technical, business, managerial, and leadership. Technical and business competencies will show the greatest distinction between SIR and MF, while Managerial and Leadership skills should be informed by company norms and expectations for people managers. Before diving into the details, I want to acknowledge that most companies have organizational designs that are not this clean or simple in practice, so you will need to make compromises to gain alignment.

Let's define the SIR day job as equally split between SQL for generating metrics, visualization tools for generating charts, and spreadsheet applications for analysis. Similarly, the MF day job is equally split between Python for implementing production-quality software, visualization tools and performance metrics for tracking model performance, and MLOps and API design for integrating with technology applications. Business competencies for both SIR and MF require strong communication, but there will be a clear bifurcation: business functional context and experience for SIR, versus technology context such as SaaS and cloud platform expertise for MF. In Step 4: Roles and Responsibilities, we will start seeing company- and industry-specific uniqueness.

Designing Roles and Responsibilities is usually a group exercise between Business, Technology, Analytics, and HR leaders. The following three considerations are grounded in personal experience from successful organizational designs and redesigns. First, adhering to company spans and layers by level titling norms (e.g., player-coach or coach managers, or Manager, Director, and VP levels). Second, rationalizing interactions and RACIs between departments is one of the most polarizing parts of the conversation, so prepare a fact base and give people time to digest before engaging on the topic. Finally, co-authorship for syndication and sponsorship is the most powerful way to get an organizational design buy in and approval.

Spans and layers define the average number of direct reports per manager, the number of organizational layers, and managerial expectations. Let's consider the expectations for coaches versus player-coaches. For example, if a manager is in a player-coach role—working as an individual contributor 50% of the time—then they should have three to five direct reports. If a manager is a coach only, they can have up to seven to ten direct reports. More direct reports are possible if managerial responsibilities are federated across tenured technical leads. There is no universal best; the design is usually guided by what is best for the company based on team size, scope of influence, budget, and talent availability. For our example, let's choose the player-coach design.

In Step 5: Working Model, we begin to decompose the individual steps needed to accomplish each process and deliverable. Take, for example, ensuring output quality. One implicit benefit of a player-coach is that the manager, who can do the technical work themselves, can also inspect and ensure the output quality standards of their direct reports. If we choose coach-only managers, we would need tenured individual contributors with the corresponding bandwidth to ensure quality standards for the rest of the team. This example shows the flexibility and cascading implications when defining roles to fulfill all responsibilities. In practice, I usually use a work cloud and Venn diagram to organize roles while ensuring completeness and minimizing gaps in the organizational design.

The next consideration is job family design. This includes estimating the number of individual contributor and managerial levels based on current and projected funding. Given we are discussing technical job families, I suggest designing a career progression that allows for longevity through both technical and managerial leadership. I typically think of a Y-shaped job family design where the entry point is the same, and after two to three levels as an individual contributor, the path splits into either technical leadership with no direct reports or managerial leadership. The Y-design allows individuals who do not want to manage others to still have long, meaningful careers. Note that this design means individual contributors may need to be compensated similarly to managers. You will need to work with HR and Finance to validate the feasibility and risk of creating such a precedent.

If a company does not allow the Y-design, the implication is an effective cap on tenure for technical staff. This is not a dealbreaker; many great departments operate without technical leadership roles. Along with HR norms, I find value in conducting market research through job boards, recruiting and consulting firms, and professional networks to validate geographic and domain norms. This is especially important when creating a new job family, expanding a team to a new geography, or competing in a tight market. For example, some international geographies expect title changes every two years, requiring nested levels. A US-based colleague might transition from Senior Data Scientist to Principal in four to six years, while an international counterpart might progress through Senior Data Scientist I, II, and III before reaching the Principal level.

Let's apply this framework to the Data Analyst and Data Scientist job families. The most fundamental design includes entry, mid, and senior levels for both Individual Contributor and People Leader roles. This usually translates into six levels. Depending on company size, these roles may only have two levels at smaller companies or five levels at larger enterprises. We will keep things simple and choose to have two levels for both Individual Contributors and People Leaders, with the latter defined as player-coaches.

The next step is to review with Human Resources and Finance. First, with HR, you must finalize job descriptions and responsibilities between levels and job families, which should inform onboarding and training materials. Roles must then be graded for compensation ranges. The final output is a job description, leveling, and compensation package that adheres to company norms. The concluding phase involves collaborating with Finance, HR, and potentially Legal to architect a transition strategy and its associated financial model. Given the inherent complexity of transition plans, it is essential to partner with HR and your Executive Sponsor to identify the most effective options for implementation.

The entire process of architecting the team, from defining skills to rationalizing a Y-shaped or linear job family design, is underpinned by three core Guiding Principles. GP 5 ("Invest and empower people") mandates the creation of durable career paths that reward technical expertise alongside managerial leadership, ensuring collective growth and retention. This design must adhere to GP 3 ("Theoretical max potential vs. ability to actualize potential"), balancing the ideal functional structure against company realities like spans, layers, and compensation norms. Finally, GP 4 ("Aim for scale") informs the Y-design and spans and layers example ratios, positioning the team for long-term growth and high throughput. In the subsequent section, we will explore a standardized framework for team staffing, including strategic guidance for managing the balance between internal and external talent acquisition.

3.2: Staffing the Team from The Ground Up

With the organizational design finalized, let's shift our focus to the critical task of staffing the team. This process involves more than just filling seats; it requires a strategic approach to sourcing, interviewing, and selecting talent that aligns with the functional charter. The following sections outline a generalized recruiting process, an iterative feedback mechanism to optimize candidate conversion, and a case study on the trade-offs between internal and external candidates.

The recruiting process is structured into three primary stages, each designed to ensure a high-performance team:

1. Sourcing: Attracting top-tier data and analytics talent in a competitive market through diverse channels.

2. Interviewing: Assessing technical proficiency and cultural fit through a structured, multi-stage evaluation.

3. Selection: Ranking candidates using a skill-gap analysis (Venn Diagram) to select individuals who maximize team outcomes.

Sourcing Strategy

Effective sourcing populates the candidate pool by focusing on quantity, quality, and throughput. To maximize quantity, job postings should be visible across company websites, professional networks like LinkedIn, internal and external job boards, and university career centers. It is often pragmatic to use attractive, external-facing titles that resonate with the market, even if they differ from internal job descriptions, which you will then explain during the interview process. I have done this before to prove the need for new titles in the HR system; sometimes you need candidates to reject a position based on titling to justify changes to HR. While this may feel inefficient, it is a very effective way to get HR aligned with a preferred design option. For most roles, a target of 50+ applicants per review cycle provides a healthy candidate pool to find a premier hire.

Relevancy and throughput are optimized by iteratively refining minimum requirements and job description wording based on early applicant reviews and feedback. If hiring for multiple similar roles, using a single "catch-all" posting prevents candidate confusion and streamlines the funnel. For senior roles with specific domain requirements (e.g., Supply Chain vs. Sales), the posting title and description must clearly articulate the unique functional experiences needed. The ultimate goal of the sourcing phase is to present five to ten highly qualified candidates per role for the initial interview round.

While numerous methodologies exist for the interview process, I want to share my personal preference—a pragmatic approach calibrated for highly competitive markets. This framework is designed to optimize candidate conversion while upholding the rigorous quality standards required for a high-performance team. I have found that a structured, three-stage process ensures a holistic evaluation of every candidate. While the specific format of subsequent interviews with business leaders and executive sponsors is often shaped by the interviewer's personal style, these additional sessions are typically reserved for the team's most senior roles and not the norm.

The Multi-Stage Interview Process:

1. Intake/Intro Call (30 mins): This initial engagement validates the candidate's baseline understanding of the role and alignment with the functional charter. It serves as a pragmatic, low-stress setting to promote the company culture and team mission. The context learned here is very helpful when trying to close an offer in a highly competitive market.

2. Background Interview (45–60 mins): This stage is a structured conversation to calibrate competencies and skills. The dialogue centers on the candidate's previous accomplishments to validate their ability to actualize potential and their aptitude for cross-functional collaboration. I usually inquire about their most challenging projects to calibrate experience and temperament against our Standard of Excellence and the unique requirements of the role. For managerial candidates, the scope expands to include their core routines for empowering and training direct reports; for leadership roles, we inquire about their ability to drive functional excellence and measurable business outcomes.

3. Technical Case Study (60 mins): This stage facilitates a simulated "Problem Solving" (PS) session, providing a venue to evaluate the candidate's ability to communicate, collaborate, and solve technical problems. Participants receive a take-home assignment specifically calibrated to their functional domain—such as

architecting a model for Data Science or deriving strategic insights for Analytics—and subsequently present their work to a panel. This collaborative presentation style gauges technical proficiency, communication efficacy, and the ability to navigate "challenger" questions or shifting constraints. For more senior roles, the insights and designs are more strategic than tactical in nature.

Selection and the Skill Venn Diagram

Final selection is guided by a team-based Venn Diagram. We assess how a candidate's specific experiences, competencies, and skills fill gaps in or complement the current team composition. For example, if hiring a manager for a new project, we might prioritize those with a proven history of recruitment and team-building over those with pure domain knowledge, as the latter can be supplemented by hiring a strong senior Individual Contributor (IC). This approach acknowledges that no candidate is perfect, but the right combination of team members ensures collective success.

Navigating Internal vs. External Candidates

When managing reorganizations or new hires, I use a 2x2 matrix of Context (business/industry knowledge) and Capabilities (technical/soft skills). Internal "High/High" candidates are "no-regrets" hires. "Low/High" (low context, high capability) individuals are similar to external hires and require onboarding and context-building time. The "High/Low" quadrant (high context, low capability) represents a significant management challenge; while these individuals may serve as viable short-term stopgaps, they will need a rigorous Personal Development Plans focused on upskilling or strategic movement to roles better suited to their profile. Although transitioning the "High/Low" group is theoretically possible, such transformations are often rare in practice due to the substantial time investment and intrinsic motivation required. Chapter 4 will cover a framework I use called Personal Development Plans to quantify the magnitude and time needed to bridge these gaps, which is very helpful for having a fact-base when navigating live conversations. I am usually open to a six-month or, infrequently, a year-long window to upskill; anything over a year is unlikely to actualize, and we look for other options. This is true for both career level and job family alignment. Finally, the "Low/Low" quadrant requires the formulation of a clear transition plan, supported by HR partnership and professional networking to facilitate placement into alternative opportunities.

Ultimately, building a new capability requires a balance of retaining institutional knowledge and injecting fresh technical expertise. While upskilling is possible, a team with more than 20–30% "low-capability" members faces a very high risk of failure. Now let's talk through Guiding Principles. Specifically, GP 3 ("Theoretical max potential vs. ability to actualize potential") is the lens through which we evaluate all candidates as we find the best fit to actualize the potential of their assigned project and team. Furthermore, this entire process is an enactment of GP 5 ("Invest and empower people"), ensuring that all staffing and upskilling decisions are strategic investments aimed at cultivating and retaining a high-performance team.

3.3: Scaling the Team while Delivering Value

This section addresses ground-level working team topics and realities. We will discuss the fine balance of delivering output while providing the necessary time for a new team to form a well-oiled, high-performance unit, a feat often accelerated through third-party staff augmentation. Next, we will cover process standardization to create output leverage. Finally, we will detail onboarding routines and norms.

Let's start with a key assumption: building the team and delivering outcomes are not mutually exclusive. Candidly, co-occurrence has a low probability without a solid game plan. My personal strategy is a mix of intentional and strategic portfolio management and resource utilization to build a Day 0 short-term, three-month roadmap to get the organization started. After Month 1 or 2, I usually have enough context about the team, business, and ecosystems to draft a higher-confidence three- to five-year long-range plan (LRP) roadmap draft for syndication, which we will discuss in depth in Chapter 5. For now, we will ground the conversation in High-Value, Low-Effort deliverables—the true "low-hanging fruit" in the classic effort-to-value 2x2 matrix. The aim is to focus on a small piece of work to give the team a high percentage chance of success at implementing the ways of working while complementing each other's skill sets to deliver output and integrate into a business process to generate business outcomes. After defining the *what*, we need to talk about the *who*. The team can be fresh new hires, existing employees, external third-party staff augmentation, or a mix of all three.

I do not believe there is a standard starter staffing model; instead, I will give more general guidance on where to focus new ways of working, and then when and how to expand to the broader team. This playbook is valid for both starting with a small group of new hires or reorganizing a large team. The key is to ensure you have a small contingency within the larger team that has the technical skills, systems understanding, and business context to get one small win on the board. If you have internal talent and context, then great. Otherwise, you will need a mix of new hires for talent or third-party staff augmentation to help bridge the gap. I usually engage third-party vendors under a Build-Operate-Transfer (BOT) Engagement Model, which is the explicit understanding to: 1) Build and Operate the technical process to generate the output and potentially process integration for business outcomes, and 2) execute a transition plan to transfer the work to an internal team to inherit the work. This BOT model concept is key when standing up a team with staff augmentation, but not necessary when leveraging staff augmentation for surge capacity. Now let's synthesize these concepts into a game plan. First, we need to find low-hanging fruit with minimal risk, non-trivial output and outcomes, and an atomic unit of a working team (skills, systems, and business context) to pilot the way of working and deliver deliverables.

Standardizing for Scale

Once we have one or two small wins under the team's belt, we can begin thinking about scaling to a larger scope via multiple concurrent workstreams. This is where we see an opportunity for standardization. I will also give one cautionary comment: You can overdo standardization. The goal is to create and define standardization that can be easily trained, implemented, and verified without distracting the team member from their main day job. For example, if you have a team with one manager and six ICs (three focused on Data Science models and three on Analytics Dashboards), standardizing roadmaps, capacity planning, and delivery cadences would be very helpful. However, standardizing coding standards via a linting tool may be overkill for the team's current maturity and scale—especially if the team is not staffed with strong software development profiles. I would rather focus on documentation and data governance; the middle ground option may be coding best practices and feedback during a routine code review. The main takeaway is to calibrate expectations of leverage with administrative overhead, allowing momentum to build over time.

Given the analytics and data product deliverables, my starter top five process standardization opportunities to create leverage are:

- Work Intake and Prioritization: How are new requests received, evaluated, and prioritized?

- Development Lifecycle: What are the stages of development, and which tools and systems should be used for deploying analytics solutions?

- Code Standards and Best Practices: How is code written, reviewed, and maintained?

- Documentation and Engagement Standards: What are the expectations for technical and user documentation or Data Cataloging? How often and what content is shared with the working team and stakeholders?

- Deployment and MLOps: How are models and solutions deployed and monitored in production?

For example, standardizing Project Intake and Prioritization can be as simple as saving a template slide deck that has skeleton pages for project scoping, roadmaps, timeline, and cost-benefits analysis. Over time, this could evolve into a set of files (slide decks and Excel worksheets) to help with leadership syndication, finance/capital budget simulations, data dictionaries, solution diagrams, and much more. Next, let's consider tooling and technology. This represents one of the toughest chasms to bridge due to the necessary technicality of the required skills. Said differently, this is where we encounter a spectrum of skills, ranging from "scrappy" practitioners to those with software engineering discipline. Scrappy team members may achieve an answer quickly, but with minimal reusability, and quality confidence will diminish as turnaround time decreases. This is not scalable or cost-effective. Leveraging Git with an Integrated Development Environment (IDE), QA checks, and a CI/CD process like MLOps will significantly increase the team's throughput, code reusability, and reduce maintenance effort. Finally, establishing Communication and Syndication routines is another major opportunity for driving throughput. This is an area where many analytics practitioners may not have had the experience or training in driving working teams, knowing how to communicate escalated requests, or facilitating a trade-off conversation to drive alignment. Having standard templates that can be filled in with a role-play practice meeting can empower junior and hyper-technical team members to engage with work teams to drive work at pace.

Onboarding for Long Term Success

Onboarding is equally important and serves as the practical application of training material for standardized processes and documentation. The incremental work needed to extend the process templates and reference material is the inclusion of instructions, which can be a mix of verbal overviews and walkthroughs, written guides and "how-tos," or even previously recorded training or knowledge-sharing sessions. I have relied on Microsoft Teams meeting records that were downloaded and stored in SharePoint as a low-budget way to generate training and onboarding videos without significant incremental effort. I personally believe onboarding can significantly impact a new hire's performance and long-term potential at a company. I think of onboarding as a Day 1, Week 1, and Month 1 plan:

- End of Day 1 - Focuses primarily on logistics like computer and/or building access and credentials.

- End of Week 1 - The new hire should know their working team, have enough context to understand the expectations for their first deliverables, and possess necessary system and data access.

- End of Month 1 - Present first-month assignment, skill assessment, and align on year-to-go deliverables.

The goal here is to set up new hires for success. Day 1 is primarily about logistics: building access, computer, and credentials. By the end of Week 1, the new hire should know their working team, have enough context to understand the expectations for their first deliverables, and possess necessary system and data access. The first month's assignment varies based on role, but given the nature of the team, I usually focus on pulling data, running pivots, identifying trends, visualizing, and presenting as a readout to the working team and manager. This allows for effectively six half-week rounds of iterations and review before the final presentation. By the end of Month 1, the top three outcomes are: 1) the new hire has enough context to discuss their year-to-go deliverables, 2) the manager has a fact base for a skills assessment and to define a Personal Development Plan, and 3) the new hire has confidence in their onboarding, team, and upcoming scope. I'll explain the Personal Development Plans in much more detail in Chapter 4. Also note, this onboarding plan can also be applied to existing employees who have transitioned from other parts of the company, and they may take less than a month to complete the initial presentation.

For completeness, I will share an observation and perspective on leveraging and engaging with contractors and third-party staff augmentation. There are trade-off considerations in time, cost, and tech debt when leveraging contractors and external capacity. Here are a couple of scenarios to consider. Let's say we have a firm helping for one month to deliver a set of analytics data assets to feed an operational scorecard. When creating a new analytics organization and its data ecosystem, you may lack a defined data and dashboard implementation standard. In this case, you may ask the firm to provide something that is more "standardized," which is effectively future tech debt. This is honestly part of the journey. The non-tech debt option would be to extend the scope to include or have a preexisting Data Strategy (Data Governance, Architecture, Engineering, and Change Management), which is well beyond the funding of a one-month dashboard engagement.

The strategy for scaling the team—by balancing quick wins with foundational growth—is fundamentally driven by three of the nine Guiding Principles. GP 7 ("Commercialize your product") prioritizes the delivery of High-Value, Low-Effort work. Simultaneously, GP 4 ("Aim for scale") mandates all standardization efforts. Finally, the structured onboarding plan is a direct execution of GP 6 ("Don't skip change management"), ensuring that members are set up for success from Day 1, which is great for long-term retention and engagement. The team has now scaled and delivered on the first 18 months of the three-year roadmap, but business needs are shifting—partially as planned and partially due to new, emergent demand. This situation is very common in businesses with dynamic business models and/or in turbulent industries. Let's discuss how to handle these situations in Section 3.4.

3.4: Evolving the Team's Charter and Design

To illustrate the practical evolution of a capability, let's explore a three-year narrative of a team's journey from a nascent analytics function to a sophisticated demand-generation powerhouse—the "Revenue Rocket" journey from Section 1.4. This story features two significant "plot twists"—the sudden need to support supply chain optimization and the emergence of a transformative technology, like GenAI—to demonstrate how to navigate shifting priorities and technological disruption.

The narrative unfolds over three distinct phases. In Year 1, the objective is to establish a foundational Strategic Insights & Reporting (SIR) capability focused on descriptive and diagnostic insights via operational dashboards. By Year 2, the mandate expands into a Model Factory (MF) to build predictive and prescriptive models that inform growth-oriented business processes. In Year 3, the goal is to integrate these models directly into digital customer and internal user experiences, achieving optimal, individualized interactions at scale.

In Year 1, we successfully onboarded an analytics team that synchronized well with business growth and technology modernization strategies. While hiring Data Scientists, we were tasked with optimizing supply chain processes due to rapid growth. This prompted HR to ask if Data Science and Operations Research required distinct organizational designs. Historically, Operations Research is the more traditional technical profile for building supply chain models when compared to Data Science. Though academically separate, companies vary in how they handle these roles; some use unique job descriptions and structures, while others group them under broader families like Advanced Analytics or Decision Science. When considering a modification to an org design—such as differentiating an Operations Research and Data Science function—I evaluate two dimensions:

1. Stakeholder Experience with Differentiation: Consider whether internal business partners can clearly distinguish between these roles and if such a distinction actually enhances their collaboration with the team.

2. Organizational Triviality: Assess the total headcount requirements. Establishing a separate job family is only a non-trivial decision if there is enough capacity—typically more than 10–15 individual contributors—to support specialized management and unique career paths.

In IT departments, the need to separate roles like Business Analyst and Technical Writer depends on team scale. Smaller teams often merge these duties, while larger ones justify differentiation. Managers may also hire hybrid profiles, allocating time across both skill sets based on experience. For our Operations Research story, we initially hired two Data Scientists with Operations Research backgrounds. Assuming the supply chain use cases delivered measurable value over the next two years, we would justify expanding the scope for a dedicated Operations Research Scientist job family with its own management layers. Ultimately, role differentiation is a matter of reaching a non-trivial scale to justify the shift. In practice, having a few team members in isolated job titles is a recipe for high turnover or comfortable complacency, which does not align with my leadership philosophy, so I don't favor this in practice. Again, this is a personal leadership philosophy design choice. Next, let's expand our example team's size and expertise to build a Model Factory.

As we expand toward a Model Factory, we inevitably encounter a second strategic pivot: the onset of a new emerging technology, Generative AI. While executive sponsors may exert pressure for rapid deployment—driven by the supposed promise of "automagically" creating exponential value—our core "Architecting the Team" playbook remains relevant for actualizing this potential. To maintain focus, we categorize GenAI use cases into three distinct archetypes: 1) Content Generation, 2) Decision Support, and 3) Automation. By prioritizing Content Generation, we can calibrate the technical requirements for Large Language Models or Diffusion Models while evaluating if the resulting organizational shift is non-trivial enough to necessitate a formal design evolution. We will delve into a more rigorous exploration of navigating AI in Chapter 5. We face a recurring and fundamental design choice: is it better to implement differentiation now or postpone that evolution? This decision depends on the scale of projects and value. We can leverage the framework above to make an informed and value-based decision.

The decision to evolve the team's design—whether by creating a distinct job family for Operations Research or GenAI—is influenced by our Guiding Principles. GP 1 ("It has to make business sense and value") and GP 3 ("Theoretical max potential vs. ability to actualize potential") ensure we only adopt a new design when the organizational scale and value justify the investment, while GP 9 ("Innovate responsibly") guides our deliberate and responsible scaling of new technologies like Generative AI, grounding innovation in ethical practice and achievable business outcomes. Having cultivated the talent and evolved the structure of the team, the final, and most critical challenge is to institutionalize the processes that ensure this performance is sustained, which is the focus of Chapter 4: Sustaining a High Performance Team.

Chapter 4: Sustaining a High Performance Team

We now shift our focus to the processes that ensure engagement, retention, and delivery, which culminates in a high-performance team. This chapter is a reflection of my personal leadership philosophy and how I approach building self-agency at scale. We will begin by extending the specificity in job families and levels to Competency, Skill, and Calibration Matrix (Section 4.1), which enables a personal inventory analysis used to build a robust Personal Development Plan (Sections 4.2). Finally, we will discuss how to extend the framework and process to Invest in Your Managers (Section 4.3). Throughout the subsections, I will share the core concepts, examples, and practical ways to implement them.

As background, I will also share the inspiration for this framework. In one of my previous roles there was an expectation to calibrate talent, and build a development plan for the top 5% talent within my department. I loved the framework and empowerment that I saw as a byproduct of the process, and I wanted to scale this process to the whole team (i.e., everyone would have a development plan). I knew I needed to evolve the process, so I enlisted the help of my mentors as thought partners to make the process scalable to my whole department. After a couple of yearly iterations I was able to increase my engagement scores to over 90%, effectively eliminate retention risks, and meet or beat department outcome targets by cultivating and sustaining a high performance team.

4.1 Competency, Skills, and Calibration Matrix

I will preemptively apologize for the permutation-heavy nature of this section, but I do believe the effort is worth the reward.

To ground our framework, we must first establish the fundamental components that serve as the bedrock of our design. I view Competencies as the link between formal Job Descriptions and the personalized development journey. In practice, I recommend a focused inventory of six to nine competencies per job family; while some may overlap across the organizational design, others remain distinctively functional. To illustrate this process, we will architect a simplified matrix centered on three core competencies for Strategic Insights and Data Science job families. The Intelligence competency serves as the bedrock for both Strategic Insights and Data Science job families. However, the application differs: an Insights Analyst requires deeper grounding in Statistical Analysis and Visualizations, whereas a Data Scientist necessitates greater proficiency in Machine Learning and Visualization. The Collaboration competency remains a shared requirement for both. While the Insights job family incorporates Process Engineering and SQL proficiency within the Implementation competency, the Data Science job family prioritizes software and solutions design paired with Python proficiency.

To further our illustrative narrative, we will now focus on the Analytics Insights Job Family by architecting the specific skills derived from our three core competencies across every level. This structured approach facilitates a comprehensive matrix encompassing two Individual Contributor and two Managerial levels, as demonstrated in Figure 1.

Figure 1: Example - Analytics Job Family Competencies and Skill matrix

	IC 1	IC 2	Mngr 1	Mng 2
Intelli gence	Skill 1: Charts & SQL	Skill 2: Problem Decomposi tion	Skill 3: KPI & Metric Design	Skill 4: Process Change Simulation s
Imple menta tion	Skill 5: Dashboard s	Skill 6: Templatize d Code	Skill 7: Reusable Products	Skill 8: Democratiz ed Products
Collab oratio n	Skill 9: Effective Communic ation	Skill 10: Drive Iterations	Skill 11: Optimize for Adoption	Skill 12: Process Redesign

The requirement for success is to ensure clarity and non-triviality between the specific skill, the level, and the core competency. As a reminder, institutionalizing this process will be an iterative journey to fully mature. The next strategic component is the *Calibration Matrix*, which represents a more sophisticated evolution of the standard skill matrix. This framework is designed to articulate the maturity of a skill as a team member continues to progress throughout their professional career cycle.

As illustrated in Figure 2, we detail the four skills within the Intelligence competency (rows) for the Analytics Job Family with the corresponding expectations (columns) across all four career levels.

Essentially, reaching a specific level means the ongoing refinement of skills from both the current and preceding stages. As you progress, the application of these abilities will evolve to meet the heightened expectations that come with more senior roles.

Figure 2: Example - Analytics Job Family Intelligence Competency Calibration matrix. Row: Skills, Columns: Expectations.

	IC 1 Exp.	IC 2 Exp.	Mngr 1 Exp.	Mng 2 Exp.
Skill 1: Charts & SQL	Implement data aggregations and visualizations	Define the correct analyst and plots	Build insights story board for syndication	Synthesis insight to drive leadership alignment
Skill 2: Problem Decomposition		Translate problem statements	Ensure enables yearly goals	Builds synergies with functional charter
Skill 3: KPI & Metric Design			Design KPI and Metrics that align with process	Navigate escalation during metric conflicts
Skill 4: Process Change Simulations				Simulation the impact of insight driven behavior changes

The Calibration Matrix was specifically designed to empower intermediate managers to support tenured ICs and direct reports with direct reports—front line and lower-level intermediate managers—by triaging and triangulating which functional skills need further maturing. This is very helpful once you get to more than 10 people managers and leaders in team size. Additionally, you will need to add incremental Skill and Calibration descriptions for people leader expectations where relevant.

For a real-world example, let's say we have 4 Job families, 8 competencies, 3 levels of IC, and 3 levels for Managers. The Competency and Skills Matrix would be 4 individual Competency and Skill matrices, like Figure 1, with 8 rows and 6 columns. Then the Calibration matrix for the team would be 32 (4 times 8) Calibration Matrices like Figure 2, with 8 rows and 6 columns with the top diagonal filled. Again, start small with just the Competency and Skill matrix, then build out the Calibration matrices based on need.

Congratulations on making it this far through the Cartesian product of combinations. Pat yourself on the back. This may seem like overkill at first, but the level of clarity gained from completing this exercise and sharing it with the team is powerful. These are a few observations from this exercise. The team is very appreciative of the accessible clarity provided by the breakdown. Each team member is now given the map, and they get to choose how fast, slow, or in-place they want to run. Managers now have a vernacular to communicate expectations and coach direct reports with more standard terminology. The matrix maintains consistency between peers and lays out the opportunities for progression.

Now for the final steps in building a calibration matrix is to calibrate the skill. The calibration process is based on the fundamental premise, "have we seen it?". When building a team, there will always be a mix of existing members, internal transfers, and external new hires. I have found it hard to calibrate based on historical accounts, so I have a strong preference to see the competency and skill demonstrated live. This is the reasoning for my framework for onboarding new team members: it ensures everyone has the same ground truth in actual and recent output and outcomes for calibration. Calibration is rather simple. We assign a classification of Proficient (P), Prior Experience (PE), Current Focus (CF), and Future Focus (FF). Proficient means we have seen the skill and can confirm mastery. Prior Experience is where there may have been previous experience but no recent opportunity to prove skill mastery. Current Focus indicates an active area of skill development. Future Focus is where the team collectively agrees there is a meaningful skill set growth opportunity. I'll show two examples below in Figure 3 and Figure 4. The first example is a fresh-out-of-school new hire as a Data Analyst (IC1), and our second profile is a recently promoted Manager 1 with five years of experience as an individual contributor and whose previous employer did not have multiple IC levels.

Figure 3: Calibration Matrix Example: Recent Graduate New Hire IC1.

	IC 1
Intelligence	Skill 1: Charts & SQL,
	IC 1 Exp: FF
Implementation	Skill 5: Dashboards
	IC 1 Exp: FF
Collaboration	Skill 9: Effective communication
	IC 1 Exp: FF

In our recent graduate example (Figure 3), we see no proficient mastery and all "Future Focus," which is standard for fresh graduates. They are trained in school with a foundational skill set to be a competitive applicant and land a job. Applicants with internships, or interns who convert to full-time employees, may have one or two proficient masteries. In our second example (Figure 4), we see a new hire Manager 1. There are a few Proficient (P) and Prior Experience (PE) classifications, but we also see a Future Focus (FF) at a lower-level expectation and a Proficient (P) classification at a higher-level expectation. All of this is expected. Keep in mind there is a reason they got the job offer: they passed the interview. The goal here is to calibrate based on the current job description, role, and company. Their previous roles and experiences will most likely not be perfectly aligned, so every calibration matrix will be unique.

Figure 4: Calibration Matrix Example: New Hire Manager 1 with one year of managerial experience and 5 years IC.

	IC 1	IC 2	Mngr 1
Intelligence	Skill 1: Charts & SQL	Skill 2: Problem Decomposition	Skill 3: KPI & Metric Design
	IC 1 Exp: P, IC 2 Exp: P, Mngr 1 Exp: FF	IC 2 Exp: C, Mngr 1 Exp: PE	Mngr. 1 Exp: FF
Implementation	Skill 5: Dashboards	Skill 6: Templatized code	Skill 7: Reusable Products
	IC 1 Exp: P, IC 2 Exp: P, Mngr 1 Exp: FF	IC 2 Exp: P, Mngr 1 Exp: PE.	Mngr. 1 Exp: FF.
Collaboration	Skill 9: Effective communication	Skill 10: Drive Iterations	Skill 11: Optimize for Adoption
	IC 1 Exp: P, IC 2 Exp: P, Mngr 1 Exp: P	IC 2 Exp: P, Mngr 1 Exp: P	Mngr. 1 Exp: P

The rigorous framework for defining and calibrating competencies and skills is a direct application of three core Guiding Principles. It is fundamentally an act of GP 5 ("Invest and empower people") by providing a clear, transparent map for personal development. By prioritizing GP 3 ("Theoretical max potential vs. ability to actualize potential") through the 'have we seen it?' calibration premise, we ensure that development is grounded in demonstrated performance, not just historical accounts. Furthermore, the structural rigor of the matrix helps the function GP 4 ("Aim for scale") by standardizing expectations across all levels and management layers. Having defined where the team is on the professional map, the next step is providing the tools and routines to facilitate the journey by leveraging the calibration chart findings to build a Personal Development Plan that ensures alignment with yearly deliverables planning and personal development focus areas in Section 4.2.

4.2 Personal Development Culture and Routines

Congratulations! We have made it through the foundational part of the journey to build a self-sustaining high-performance team. Next, let's discuss the process of collating the calibration matrix insights into a Personal Development Plan (PDP). We need to acknowledge a fundamental assumption to our process. There is clarity in a yearly roadmap and upcoming work. Keep in mind the roadmap can be very explicit like build an operation score card for department A, or a predictive model with Next Best Action for persona B, or high level like support a fleet of analytics models and processes for incremental improvement or product breaks for all of IT. We will soon see why this clarity is crucial.

Let's get back to our reference framework, the next component is reference journeys. Given that a reasonable expectation is for team members to achieve Proficient classification for an average of 2 to 3 skill set focus areas in a year, the reference journey acts as a template project plan. It strategically maps the sequence of skill set focus areas and example projects required to confirm skill mastery through each Job Family level. We must keep in mind that progression depends on an individual's capabilities, available funding, and company needs/opportunities, meaning Reference Journeys are strictly a starting point and must be tailored to the individual. The next topic is acknowledging the duration and number of repetitions required before reaching skill set mastery.

Building and updating visualizations may involve weekly iterations. A team member could complete ~10 visualization projects in a year to reach Proficiency classification in designing highly effective dashboards, with confirmation based on user feedback on insight quality and outcome enablement. However, building a reusable product and validating application and reusability, such as standardizing functional department scorecards, could take a year or two to design, generalize, and implement across multiple functional units before confirming Proficiency. The expectations are high at more senior levels and deliverables take longer in time. This is because the latter project requires adoption, governance, and executive alignment throughout each iteration with a feedback loop for cascading improvement as your scale across multiple functional areas. Again the reference journey is just a thought starter, and each person, project, and scope will have its own variation. Through building the reference journey, you may notice synergies between skills that will naturally coincide based on output needs to exemplify those skills. This grouping will naturally help break up the journeys between yearly planning cycles.

With the Reference Journeys established, we can use our Calibration matrix results to sequence skill set focus areas into a multi-year journey for person development. For our simple example of three competencies, mastery could and should be reached in one year. In a more realistic Competency and Skills matrix with eight competencies, going from a Level 1 to 2 IC will typically take three years (e.g., three skills in Year 1, two in Year 2, and the final three in Year 3). While some highly-driven team members complete four skills in a year, this is a function of internal motivation, life flexibility, and intrinsic desire to consume training and coaching; it is not the average or common expectation. The next step in our process is incorporating the identified skill set focus areas into our year end routines. From here, we build a game plan that gives team members clarity on work alignment, formal training, and the supporting community required to actualize the plan and realize the results.

The Personal Development Plan is the final output of this process, which has 5 key components: Focus Statement, Projects & Opportunities, Training, Feedback and Coaching Network, and SMART Goals for Confirmation. The Focus Statement is a simple "one-liner" sentence to frame the development focus, ensuring alignment and clarity. Projects & Opportunities must align with yearly deliverables and resource allocation. This is how managers validate feasibility across roadmaps and successfully create development opportunities. Aligning work with personal development is a force multiplier for engagement and quality, answering the critical "What's in it for me?" question. At times, this means shuffling team members between projects and teams, which keep team members engaged and prevent stagnation. The Training section should include references to formal curriculums, certifications, books, or other materials. While training budgets are beneficial, a highly motivated person will always find free training content online. The key is for team members to be prepared before committing to skill set focus areas. Team members must specify a Feedback and Coaching Network - individuals who will intentionally provide support on a topic. This ensures the Personal Development Plan remains active beyond the first month. Depending on the skill and level, this may require explicitly engaging team members outside the department to confirm their willingness and availability to share feedback. Finally, SMART Goals for Confirmation answer the question: "How will we know?" There should be clear expectations on the output and outcomes used to formally confirm skill Proficiency.

I have found that institutionalizing the PDP process is, at minimum, a two-year journey. During year 1, we focused on architecting a simplified skill matrix and foundational Personal Development Plans, allowing for iterative refinements through subsequent yearly feedback cycles. By the fifth year, we successfully scaled this into a robust, department-level Competency Matrix, complete with job-family-specific skills and calibration matrices. At this level of maturity, I empowered my front-line and intermediate managers to own their respective review cadences before I conducted a final review. To effectively "inspect with respect," I established a routine of quarterly progress updates to maintain our Standard of Excellence. My advice is to remain pragmatic and start small; your framework will naturally evolve to align with the team's shifting needs and business cycles. The final consideration is the long-term motivation for the PDP.

I intentionally prioritize the concept of *progression* over promotion, as the Personal Development Plan is designed to facilitate any form of career advancement, whether through vertical movement or a strategic transition. Connecting back to section 3.2, this framework provides the data-driven foundation needed to quantify the investment required for a career pivot, enabling a pragmatic balance between the decision to upskill internal candidates or recruit external talent. Regarding advancement, I adhere to a specific leadership philosophy: we promote based on a candidate's potential for success in the next role, while rewarding high performance in the current role through yearly performance reward mechanisms. Because promotion cycles are often a function of external factors like funding and organizational need, I explicitly decouple the PDP from the formal promotion process. My ultimate goal is to empower every team member to actualize their theoretical max potential, regardless of their eventual destination. To put it simply: I am a developer and exporter of talent. I find success in cultivating a deep bench of high-potential individuals who can drive impact across the enterprise or beyond. I saw this in a few of my managers and mentors over the years, and it forever influenced my leadership philosophy.

The Personal Development Plan framework is embodiment of GP 5 ("Invest and empower people"), providing a transparent, structured pathway for continuous professional growth. By quantifying the investment needed for career pivots and separating progression from formal promotion, the process rigorously upholds GP 3 ("Theoretical max potential vs. ability to actualize potential"). Finally, the PDP process actualizes GP 2 ("Everyone is a change agent") by empowering each team member to reach their full potential as a Change Agent. Crucially, the entire system relies on the consistent execution and coaching capabilities of the department's people leaders. Therefore, we must focus on extending this framework in Section 4.3 to Invest in your Managers.

4.3: Invest in Your Managers

While many exceptional managerial frameworks and guides exist, I want to share the high-level framework I employ in practice to develop leadership talent. This section details how this framework serves as a yearly training series and how I leverage an apprenticeship model to create leadership opportunities through coaching and structured routines.

To ground this framework for more tenured readers, imagine yourself in a management role where you still engage tactically, perhaps leading individual contributors or managing a small department. It is built around five core managerial competencies: Expectation Setting, Performance Enablement, Communication Cadence, Capability Evaluation, and Team Culture. The motivation and framing for each managerial competency was to empower people leaders with a set of tactical actions they could leverage to activate the team to reach its full potential and expected outcomes. I'll give one quick example of how I bring this to life when introducing the framework to team members for the first time: new hire onboarding. If you recall, I have the End of Day 1, End of Week 1, and End of Month 1 game plan for new hires in Chapter 3.2. I use this scenario to highlight how powerful the managerial framework is by detailing what each task would be for the new hire onboarding scenario to maximize their potential success while preventing common pitfalls.

Managerial Competencies

Expectation Setting begins with breaking down the work by mapping out the project into small, sequential steps and milestones, such as securing system access and planning the final presentation. You must then define success by explaining the distinction between the thing you build (the output) and the result you want (the outcome), while creating a simple timeline for the initial onboarding weeks. It is pragmatic to ensure the hire knows who to work with for data context and review iterations, while setting priorities through routine check-ins to rebalance the plan as issues arise.

To drive Performance Enablement, cultivate a habit of checking In with open-ended, non-judgmental questions to gauge progress. When the team member drifts, focus on gently course-correcting with high-impact advice and removing roadblocks like system issues or engagement conflicts immediately. Success is achieved by solving problems together, working side-by-side to analyze feedback and iterate on next steps.

Establishing a robust Communication Cadence requires explaining the "why" behind assignments to show how they fit the bigger picture. You should review progress through regular focused work sessions and provide dedicated coaching time via weekly one-on-ones. Additionally, collecting honest feedback from outside the team and ensuring the new hire is making personal connections with collaborators helps them build strong, professional relationships beyond mere titles.

For Capability Evaluation, you must create observation opportunities for their interaction with peers while reviewing the work technically to gauge current skills and opportunities. This evaluation is bolstered by gathering 360-degree input from leaders and peers and using peers' observations to assess the hire's grasp of internal systems and tools.

Finally, sustaining Team Culture involves connecting work to a purpose so the impact on company goals is clear, and building trust by soliciting feedback on the onboarding process. You should establish team habits like planning and code reviews while fostering inclusion through interest groups. Ultimately, focusing on retention means providing a clear Personal Development Plan and a transparent explanation of your leadership philosophy while addressing any issues.

Training Process

We reinforce and apply this framework through a series of bi-weekly, 60-minute training sessions designed to drive functional excellence. To ensure psychological safety, we establish a "Trust Tree" environment—an explicit agreement that our dialogues remain confidential, non-judgmental, and focused on abstracting lessons to maintain our Standard of Excellence. We initiate the journey with a 90-minute kickoff to review the framework and invite managers to share their interpretations of each competency and ideate on tactical tasks. Central to these sessions is a two-part case study template: the left side of the page captures the issue's context and the tactical steps taken, while the right side documents alternative actions and their expected outcomes. By cycling through two topics per session, everyone gets a chance to engage and reflect on their own scenarios and brainstorm to help others over a six-month cycle, providing the bandwidth to internalize the concepts and implement them with their respective working teams.

To move beyond standard training routines, I implement an apprenticeship model designed to institutionalize mentorship capabilities at scale. I empower managers to architect and lead internal interest committees—such as Lunch-and-Learns, Code Reviews, Yearly Training, or the Experimentation Committee—to create a self-sustaining loop of professional growth. My role is to coach the committee lead on how to define a vision and empower others, rather than personally managing the operational details. For example, a manager leading the Lunch-and-Learn committee must align the technical curriculum with the team's individual Personal Development Plans to ensure each session acts as a force multiplier for the group. They are responsible for auditing content and coaching presenters to ensure development goals are reached. As the functional capability matures, these managers mentor senior individual contributors to assist with content preparation, facilitating a cascade of mentorship that ensures the department's leadership capacity evolves organically and sustainably.

This entire managerial development routine—from the structured training sessions to the apprenticeship model—is a crucial mechanism for institutionalizing our core guiding principles. By leveraging the framework, we ensure a sustainable leadership pipeline, GP 5 ("Invest and Empower People"). Furthermore, the focus on coaching and scaling mentorship capacity is the most effective way to institutionalize effective change management, GP 6 ("Don't skip change management"), ensuring every people leader is equipped to drive transformation with empathy, clarity, and empowerment. Having established the robust systems for cultivating and sustaining a high-performance team (Chapters 3 and 4), our final focus shifts from internal operations to external delivery. Chapter 5: Evolving the Capability with Business Needs will detail the strategic processes for converting our team's potential into quantifiable outcomes by mastering work intake, roadmapping, and the use case life cycle.

Chapter 5: Evolving the Capability with Business Needs

This chapter shifts our focus to the practical work of scoping and delivering output and, most critically, ensuring we convert those outputs into measurable outcomes. While traditional analytics focuses heavily on the mathematical aspects of building insights and models, we will highlight two "superpower" skill sets—Process Engineering and Managerial Accounting—that are essential force multipliers for driving true business outcomes. Process Engineering enables practitioners to turn an analytical *insight* into a measurable *action* by defining specific changes to user experiences. Managerial Accounting allows practitioners to build financial models that quantify and track actions to their ultimate financial outcomes. Together, these skills empower the practitioner to design, quantify, and validate business value, closing the loop on ROI and strategic impact. This becomes the inspiration for our "5 Insights to Impact" questions, providing a framework for building a commercially viable roadmap (Section 5.1). We then explore the steps for building analytics products through the Use Case Lifecycle (Section 5.2: Prep, Pilot, Production). Finally, we demonstrate how to generalize and extend this lifecycle for new and emerging technologies, with a focus on Generative AI (Section 5.3), ensuring that innovation remains grounded in achievable business value.

5.1 Work Intake and Roadmaps

I favor frameworks because they ensure a concise, consistent, and configurable process that teams can be trained on at scale. For work intake, I use another framework, the "5 Insights to Impact Questions," inspired by the "5 Whys" concept in root cause analysis. These five questions serve as my guiding star when conducting discovery to frame a problem, design a solution, and drive impact. Question 1—"What is the right analytical output or 'Engine'?"— focuses on what we are planning to build, ensuring coverage and quality. Question 2—"Who is the user, and in which systems and workflows will they use this output?"—centers on process and user mapping. This is critical for defining the scope of systems and users, as well as accurately estimating technical implementation and change management costs. The subsequent questions clarify the future state and provide traceability: Question 3—"How will the insight change the user's action?"—defines the shift in behavior; Question 4—"How does this new action change the established business process?"—links that action to the macro business process; and Question 5—"How does the change in the process translate into P&L impact?"—quantifies the financial ROI (or ROIC for portfolio management).

A quick note on sequencing: Due to my engineering background, I always think of solutions flowing from Insight to Impact (1 to 5). More classically trained business profiles will often use the opposite sequence, working back from the desired Impact to Insight (5 to 1). Both sequencing methods are equally valid. In practice, when driving innovation through emerging technology, I will start with the insight and then map the impact; when I am driving commercial growth strategies, I will work back from the impact to identify the required insights.

To illustrate, consider a Customer Lifetime Value (CLV) use case from our Revenue Rocket scenario. Question 1: "What is the right analytical output or 'Engine'?" Here, it is the identification of key signals indicating a major drop-off in product usage, paired with a preemptive decline prediction. Question 2: "Who is the user, and in which systems will they use this output?" Inside Sales reps will access these insights within the CRM to manage proactive customer engagement. Question 3: "How will the insight change the user's action?" This output enables better customer prioritization and improves the first-call resolution rate. Question 4: "How does this new action change the established business process?" The updated approach transforms a reactive workflow into a proactive outreach tool for boosting net CLV. Finally, Question 5: "How does the change translate into P&L impact?" Extending the average customer lifespan directly fuels revenue growth through retention, creating a measurable result on the P&L. Based on these answers, we can define project scope, required teams, timelines, costs, and the measurable effect on operating income.

A critical consideration—often relegated to an *afterthought* yet posing a substantial risk to actualizing a net ROI—is the Total Cost of Ownership (TCO) and ongoing operational expenditure. This encompasses both long-term technology and sustained resourcing costs; even an exceptional product delivered within an 18-month window must account for the economic realities of Month 19 and beyond. Additionally, establishing long-term accountability before we start the project is a must: we must determine if the product will transition into base operational capacity post launch or requires incremental resources during the initial planning.

Roadmap Prioritization and Deconfliction

The next step is to work through the list of project requests, scope out work of reasonable value to complete a discovery, stack-rank the projects, and then draw a line of capacity to rationalize what is above or below the line of funded capacity. Projects deemed "must-do" move to the top of the list, and their capacity is removed from the "up for debate" list for above-the-line rationalization. I will share a cautionary tale: Disconnects can happen when one business leader claims a project is a high priority and a must-do, but the collective senior leadership is not aligned. If possible, try to conduct a quick, low-touch discovery and commercial validation, and let the numbers speak for themselves. Or communicate to your manager and let the appropriate levels handle the feedback. This is where things start getting political, and, naturally, this is part of the job and process that happens every year.

An intermediate step is often required between directional and finalized alignment to deconflict and validate resourcing. Once we have mapped out teams, budgets, and estimated timelines, we must overlay all capacity and deployment windows to avoid conflicts. For example, if a data team is expected to support two major integrations concurrently, the de-risked option is concurrent development with staggered production launches. We must also account for holidays and major customer events, such as avoiding a major product launch during the peak holiday purchasing season. These steps can be administratively burdensome, but project management software can lessen the load. The key is to give each team lead an opportunity to validate feasibility once a complete integrated roadmap is drafted. This effort is worth its weight in gold, as it is far easier to make edits during the final alignment phase than to walk back a timeline once implementation has begun.

The "5 Insights to Impact Questions" framework serves as the operational mechanism for several Guiding Principles, most notably GP 1 ("It has to make business sense and value") and GP 8 ("Objective vs. Utility function"), by forcing a rigorous connection between technical work and financial outcomes. This structured approach to discovery and prioritization ensures that every roadmap initiative is calibrated to actualize potential GP 3 ("Theoretical max potential vs. ability to actualize potential") while building engines that are ready to be commercialized GP 7 ("Commercialize your product"). With the roadmap aligned and prioritized, we now turn our attention to the standardized execution model for bringing these initiatives to life: the Use Case Lifecycle.

5.2: Use case Lifecycle

The use case lifecycle provides a standardized framework for the "living organism" of work. This model emerged from a need to scale operations across a growing team of new hires and diverse stakeholders. While specific details vary by project type, these three core phases - Prep, Pilot, and Production - are generalizable across dashboards, analytical models, and full-scale digital transformations. This structure facilitates a feedback loop of lessons learned and observations to refine future uses.

Phase 1: Prep

Phase 1 focuses on validating scope, discovery, feasibility, and proof of value. While high-level scoping occurs during intake, the Prep phase requires dedicated, full-time focus to "measure twice and cut once." The team is organized into two concurrent workstreams: Group 1 addresses users, processes, and financial modeling, while Group 2 focuses on data, technology, and intelligence. The primary outputs are a Change Management Playbook from Group 1 and a Product Requirements Document from Group 2, providing the detail necessary to confirm discovery completion for process and technical implementation.

Feasibility is assessed by asking, "What needs to be true?", which is an extremely powerful and empowering question for identifying hidden dependencies or scope gaps. This leads to the "Paper Pilot," like printing out a spreadsheet for someone to review, a proof-of-value step where synthetic or actual data is used to create sample outputs. By sharing these samples with end users, we validate if the insights are valuable in facilitating the intended business decisions before committing to full development.

Phase 2: Pilot

The Pilot phase consists of technical implementation, product performance management, and initial rollout. During implementation, the team activates software licenses, builds data integrations and infrastructure, and curates governance policies. Technology partners should help identify the right tools and solutions within the internal landscape using reference architectures. Product performance management then establishes metrics to monitor the user experience, analytics quality, and system resilience, ensuring we identify issues before the end user does.

The initial rollout bridges the gap between technical implementation and user adoption. Learning and Development (L&D) strategies are tailored to the persona: external customers may receive demo videos, while internal employees undergo change management training to transition from old routines to new data-driven processes. A clear feedback mechanism ensures that no user is left frustrated during this transition, and there is a clear method to federate feedback to the appropriate team for resolution.

Phase 3: Production

Once the pilot has resolved technical bugs and process quirks, the team proceeds to full-scale Production. This phase involves transition planning, scale-out with hyper-care, and long-term continuous improvement. Transitioning from a project team to a permanent support team is critical; while some staff may roll off, a core contingency may persist to manage the product in perpetuity.

During scale-out, "hyper-care" support manages the influx of new users, leveraging lessons and FAQs from the pilot. Always remember to run your pilot pre-flight and post-flight checks before deploying to new segments as part of scale-out. The final step is managing incremental features and integrations with other functional capabilities that create synergies and compound the engine's value over time. This ensures the product remains relevant and continues to drive measurable business outcomes.

Once the transition to the permanent team occurs, they will then focus on building a feature roadmap for continuous improvements and adjacencies. For small-scale projects like a dashboard there may be a general backlog for the team supporting all dashboards, and they can take feedback and prioritize against all other supported dashboards. When thinking of large-scale projects and products with a dedicated team, they will want to build their own focused roadmap of features requested by users for continued improvements or incremental work and integrations with other functional capability to create leverage and synergies.

The use case lifecycle is operationalized through a continuous feedback loop, occurring either during or after a project's completion. This iterative process integrates lessons learned and identifies necessary procedural refinements. For instance, it may involve formalizing a roster of reference teams to consult based on specific technology platforms or user groups, or adapting to varied departmental coordination styles—ranging from rigorous "Air

Traffic Control" (ATC) protocols for deployment to the formal weekly status meeting for end user awareness. I have effectively utilized this lifecycle as a mechanism for onboarding new personnel and assisting team members in navigating stakeholder transitions when moving between projects. Moreover, the lifecycle serves as a strategic tool for scope management by establishing clear stage-gate reviews for working teams and both first-line and intermediate managers. The people leaders can use the lifecycle to align on steps towards completion, selection stage gate points, and schedule check in to empower the team with self agency and autonomy with metered length of a project.

The use case lifecycle is operationalized through a continuous feedback loop, occurring either during or after a project's completion. This iterative process integrates lessons learned and identifies necessary procedural refinements. For instance, it may involve formalizing a roster of reference teams to consult based on specific technology platforms or user groups, or adapting to varied departmental coordination styles—ranging from rigorous "Air Traffic Control" (ATC) protocols for deployment to the formal weekly status meeting for end user awareness.

Finally, I will share a few creative ways to leverage the Use case Lifecycle in other team routines. I have effectively utilized this lifecycle as a mechanism for onboarding new personnel and assisting team members in navigating stakeholder transitions when moving between projects. Additionally, the lifecycle serves as a strategic tool for scope management by establishing clear stage-gate reviews for working teams and both first-line and intermediate managers. The people leaders can use the lifecycle to align on steps towards completion, selected stage-gate points, and schedule check-ins to empower the team with self-agency and autonomy with defined project durations. The structured execution of the Use Case Lifecycle is a direct application of GP 7 ("Commercialize your product"), ensuring every technical output is developed with the operational rigor and maintenance standards required of a business-ready engine. By instituting standardized phases and feedback loops, the framework also satisfies GP 4 ("Aim for scale"), creating a modular and repeatable delivery model that minimizes technical debt as the portfolio grows. This lifecycle, while foundational for traditional analytics and data science, provides the essential framework for navigating the unique complexities and rapid evolution of Generative AI, which we will explore in Section 5.3.

5.3: Extending the Use Case Life Cycle for Generative AI

Congratulations on reaching this seminal section. For those who jumped straight to this topic, let's get to it and establish a clear, actionable path forward. The key idea here is not to skip foundational steps for the excitement of a new technology.

This framework outlines a maturity curve of incremental wins required to successfully build an AI capability. The progression moves from solidifying data product commercialization to strategic integration:

- Win 1 - Foundational Value: Drive measurable business value (e.g., 1% revenue growth, margin expansion, or cost optimization) using traditional data products.
- Win 2 - Capacity and Experimentation: Build the capacity and capability to successfully experiment with AI use cases.
- Win 3 - Strategic Fit: Determine where and how AI—from a technical and ethical standpoint—makes long-term business sense for your company then execute.

Win 1: Foundational Value

Whether you select 1% in Revenue growth or margin expansion is inconsequential; the goal is to prove to the team and the company the capability of commercializing and communicating data products to drive outcomes, even just once. Begin with basic KPI and operational metric insights to inform strategic and tactical decisions. This builds a foundation in data platforms and governance while providing experience in change management and user adoption. Next, expand into Machine Learning, where insights may have less explainability than arithmetic-based metrics, and outputs are no longer tied to accounting principles (e.g., recommendation systems, customer lifetime value growth, or optimized warehouse selection paths). The sheer throughput of these outputs will necessitate building the next level of governance and change management experience. Finally, recognize that the necessary technology platforms and products will naturally emerge as part of this journey. Hit 1% incremental value through data products, and you will gain the context needed to successfully drive value with AI.

Win 2: Capacity and Experimentation

Assuming you have successfully accomplished Win 1, you are now ready to experiment with AI, focusing first on Generative use cases. Remember, Language Models predict the letters in the next word, and Diffusion Models predict the RGB values of the next pixel. You should use a forecasting model for forecasting problems.

Look at your business model to identify low and high-value use cases for creating text and/or image-based content. For e-commerce, product descriptions, reviews, and images are excellent starting points. Be aware that the governance required for text and images will be very different and demand incremental investment. On the technical side, start simple: use commercially available hosted endpoints for a frontier model to get the use case launched, and optimize later. The goal is to get wins on the board and let successful use cases influence future decisions.

Depending on your business model and customer base, Generative use cases may not drive large-scale value, and automation may be the true value driver. Here, I suggest experimenting with a bridging set of use cases focused on Decision Support to optimize process throughput before concluding Win 2. Decision support occurs when a person conducts the process and owns the final decision, leveraging AI to enhance the workflow, while full automation involves only automated processing operating with defined guardrails without human intervention.

Take a customer support call center agent, for example. We can build an AI solution that collates data from multiple sources (leveraging an established Customer 360 data set in a Customer Data Platform, or CDP). This "Generative" capability can streamline the process by providing a summary of potential customer issues through historical insights and suggested resolutions. This is still decision support, but it optimizes handling times, which equates to reduced wait times and more customer issues resolved per work hour. The V1.1 of this use case would involve integrating predictive and prescriptive models as context to be incorporated into the Gen AI output, which would help improve conversion and resolution rates. These use cases can often be accomplished with commercially hosted models, prompt engineering, and staged feature stores such as a NoSQL database or Retrieval Augmented Generation (RAG), if you really feel the need. The point here is that you don't need an established AI engineering department to start and learn. Don't over complicate things at this stage.

Reinforcing the groundwork: bypassing Win 1 jeopardizes these applications, as success depends on pre-existing capabilities for data access, insight quality, and the seamless integration of findings into systems like Contact Center Software. Skipping foundational steps does not save time; it merely compromises outcomes. Furthermore, I contest the common belief that Generative AI requires more rigorous Data Governance than traditional Machine Learning models. While some view this as a novel demand, maintaining a high standard of excellence has always been essential for deploying high fidelity insights at scale. The real transformation is Gen AI's unprecedented accessibility: a lower barrier to entry increases both the opportunity for organizational empowerment and the peril of poor oversight. This difference is evident in the capture of process and contextual metadata; while machine learning models often require logical translation for inputs, Generative AI processes more conventional data. Historically, the business logic within that logical process served as the governance for conversational context. Having successfully developed the capacity and actualized the value of Win 2, the next critical step is moving toward Win 3 to establish a strategic fit for AI within your long-term business goals.

Win 3: Strategic Fit

In Win 3, we tackle the most important long-term question: how does AI make sense for our company, business model, and customer experience? I prefer to frame this conversation from the customer experience perspective, determining where and when we should enable automation. I leverage a pragmatic 2x2 framework rooted in the Empathy Premium (High vs. Low) and Intelligence Integration (Automation vs. Decision Support) to architect an enterprise-scale AI investment strategy.

The framework for enterprise-scale AI investment is structured around the two dimensions of Empathy Premium (High vs. Low) and Intelligence Integration (Decision Support vs. Full Automation). Solutions requiring a high Empathy Premium—where a person must be involved—fall into two categories: *Consultative Partnership* for complex problems requiring human expertise, Decision Support, and AI insights (e.g., Financial planning), or *Empathetic Resolution* for simple problems where a customer needs a human "ear" and Full Automation (e.g., a service recovery conversation for a late delivery). For use cases with a low Empathy Premium (e.g., filling out a form), the solutions are *Expert Systems* for deep technical tasks a human, with Decision Support, just wants done right by a machine (e.g., Tax calculation), or *Self-Service Utility* for Full Automation of basic, low-stakes transactions (e.g., changing a password or tracking a package). For the majority of use cases, Prompt and RAG-based AI solutions deliver significant short-term outcomes with minimal investment. Domain-specific Fine-Tuning serves to bridge remaining performance gaps for specialized context or cost optimization. Finally, Ground-up Custom Models are rarely the best option for most and should only be pursued if justified by unique business constraints or value.

By utilizing this 2x2 matrix, we can effectively organize specific AI use cases to a quadrant, which will correlate to a solution and/or team to convert technical output to business outcomes. This strategic alignment allows for the precise quantification of investment budgets and the federated execution of projects across internal departments and external partners. Depending on your organization's unique technological landscape and existing maturity, this framework directs initiatives towards an internal "Build" path through specialized units—whether that be a Robotic Process Automation team, the scientific wing of an Analytics department, or a dedicated AI engineering function. For many other organizations, the optimal path is "Buy", which involves integrating SaaS-based AI solutions while managing the necessary technical architecture and process reengineering. Following this calibration, we move into a standard intake and roadmapping phase, now supported by enhanced governance and strict resource alignment to fully realize the portfolio's potential.

In summary, these three wins—foundational value, capacity for experimentation, and strategic fit—and their sequential execution represent my thesis statement on the successful architecture of AI Capability Building. This structured progression ensures that the organization does not merely chase emerging technology but builds a self-sustaining ecosystem where every technical advancement is anchored in measurable business outcomes. The decision to commit to this intentional path is governed by my nine guiding principles (GP 1–9), which ensure the successful execution of the three wins: Foundational Value, Capacity and Experimentation, and Strategic Fit. Foundational Value is secured by adhering to GP 1 ("It has to make business sense and value") and GP 7 ("Commercialize your product"), ensuring every output is a commercialized engine that provides measurable business sense and value, quantified using GP 8 ("Objective vs. Utility function") to actualize potential, GP 3 ("Theoretical max potential vs. ability to actualize potential"). Capacity and Experimentation is built by committing to GP 5 ("Invest and empower people") and GP 6 ("Don't skip change management") while GP 4 ("Aim for scale") in the design of the AI capability. Finally, Strategic Fit ensures sustainable long-term value, GP 1 ("It has to make business sense and value") by GP 9 ("Innovate responsibly") and GP 2 ("Everyone is a change agent") to continuously prioritize the actualization of business value (GP 3) over theoretical ideals. By adhering to this framework, leadership can move beyond the "pilot purgatory" that often stalls digital transformations. This approach facilitates a rigorous calibration of technical capabilities against organizational maturity, ensuring that as the team matures from Strategic Insights to Model Factories and eventually into Innovation and Research, the governance and technical rigor scale in tandem. Ultimately, this methodology converts AI from a speculative investment into a commercialized engine for business process transformation and sustainable financial growth.

Outro

Congratulations! If you have followed the framework from Chapter 1 through 5, you have successfully learned the foundational steps for establishing a high-performance, modern data and analytics function. You have transformed a simple mandate into a durable capability—one designed to cultivate talent, operate seamlessly, and evolve with the pace of technology. However, Capability Building is not a project with a defined end date; it is a continuous journey. The true test of your efforts is to convert the individual components we have built into a self-reinforcing system that drives continuous growth: The Capability Building Flywheel.

The core of this book is directly aligned with a growth flywheel strategy and has been structured around the four vertical pillars of Capability Building: Designing the Capability (Chapter 2), Cultivating a Team (Chapter 3), Sustaining a High Performance Team (Chapter 4), and Evolving the Capability with Business Needs (Chapter 5). When these pillars are activated and linked together, they create a continuous flywheel of business value that requires less external energy over time.

1. Designing the Capability (Chapter 2): The cycle begins by translating the strategic vision into an actionable functional charter and organizational blueprint, setting the foundation for all staffing and development.

2. Cultivating a Team (Chapter 3): Designing, staffing, and developing talent via the calibration matrix and PDPs create engaged, high-capacity individuals with the skills to deliver.

3. Sustaining a High Performance Team (Chapter 4): The implementation of management routines and processes ensures consistent, reliable delivery, creating proven value that justifies continued investment in the team.

4. Evolving the Capability with Business Needs (Chapter 5): The sustained value creation provides the financial and organizational capacity to strategically innovate with new technologies (like Gen AI) and secure the next cycle of funding, driving long-term priorities.

This continuous loop ensures that every successful outcome drives further investment in the people and processes, leading to an accelerated rate of capability maturity. Crucially, the ultimate result of this flywheel is the continuous production and commercialization of new analytical Engines, ensuring the capability is always driving durable, value-added business transformation.

The principles and frameworks shared in this book are designed to serve as your field manual. You do not need a perfect organizational design or unlimited resources to begin. You only need to choose one small process—one team routine, one onboarding step, or one use case—apply the concepts, watch what happens, and learn from it.

The journey of capability building begins with a single step. I hope this book empowers you to take that first step to drive meaningful business transformation.

Cheers,

Majid

Appendix: Unsolicited Advice

This Appendix is framed as a Q&A session following a capability building presentation. The advice is segmented by career level, responding to the final question: "What is the single most important piece of guidance you can share, given my current career level?"

The following "Unsolicited Advice" for each career level serves as a direct, personalized application of the nine Guiding Principles (GP) established in Section 1.3, designed to translate philosophical guidance into actionable career steps.

- The Individual Contributor (A.1): Focuses on personal execution and achieving outcomes (GP 3, 7, 8).

- The First Line Manager (A.2): Focuses on capability transfer and mentorship (GP 5, 6).

- The Intermediate Manager (A.3): Focuses on empowering and scaling coaching (GP 2, 5).

- The Department Lead (A.4): Focuses on transformation, strategy, and change management (GP 1, 6, 9).

- The Executive Sponsor (A.5): Focuses on strategic investment and organizational design (GP 1, 4, 9).

A.1: The Individual Contributor

A few years ago, I was giving a presentation to a group of graduate students. During that conversation, I shared a simple framework I use to think about job transitions and career development when starting out. I break the journey into three phases:

1. Phase 1: The Paycheck. The immediate goal is to calculate the minimum salary you need to make your life sustainable. Solve for the minimum, and everything else is a pleasant treat.

2. Phase 2: The Job. After a year or two, you will start recognizing what you genuinely enjoy or dislike. This helps you transition from a "paycheck" role to a job that you actually like and enjoy.

3. Phase 3: The Career. This phase is tightly linked to you finding long-term growth, sustainability, and personal fulfillment out of that role. This is where you plant roots to grow a career.

After sometime you will start thinking about progression and growth. My universal framework for progression is to understand the distinction and evolution from an Individual Contributor to an Independent Contributor.

Initially, as an Individual Contributor, someone is helping you every step of the way. Progression comes when you transition to being fully independent. This means you can manage yourself, possess the competencies and skills to engage team members, and reliably deliver your output. When you start successfully managing yourself as an Independent Contributor, that is where progression—whether to greater seniority as an IC or moving into a management role—begins to happen.

A.2: The First Line Manager

You were highly successful as an Individual then Independent Contributor, and now you are managing your first team. Congratulations!

The most important thing to realize is the difference between you *knowing how to do the skill* versus you *teaching somebody how to do the skill*. There's a theory around expert systems around "chunking," where you skip steps because you have built unconscious recognition on how to complete a task. When you are managing people for the first time, you have to remind yourself to go back to first learning the skill and breaking down your thought process to atomic units to teach someone.

I always give people this classic example regarding visualizations: if you show somebody a visualization and they give you feedback that they don't understand it, how do you start decomposing what they don't understand? Is it the numbers, the trend, something counterintuitive between the plot type versus the analysis hypothesis, or the colors? As you're coaching somebody, the real key is learning how to break down the "I don't know" into specific updates to the visualization.

I think of coaching and managing like the double-sided Mexican bingo card, Loteria: for every technical or business skill you have, there is an equivalent flip side to that card. The first side is: yes, you can do the skill. The second side is: can you mentor somebody to build that skill? That's something many first-time managers don't realize—there's a second set of competencies that is not you doing the task, but you coaching the task.

When I think about the act of coaching, I usually break the process down into Watch One, Do One, Lead One. If I'm training somebody on a skill, the process is: Watch One, where they observe me complete one full iteration; Do One, where the direct report does the task while I coach them step-by-step, providing intermediate feedback; and finally Lead One, where they lead the iteration fully independently to demonstrate mastery. I emphasize 1, 2, 3 as a conceptual guide; it may take more iterations, but the concept remains: successfully show them, help them do it, and finally, have them execute independently. This is the path to mastery.

A.3: The Intermediate Manager

When you transition into an intermediate manager role—where your direct reports are managers with direct reports, potentially two, three, or four levels removed—the key challenge shifts. You can no longer coach the individual contributors or managers directly. You must learn what it means to coach by proxy or indirectly.

Your primary focus becomes developing your team members through observational opportunities and role-playing. You can set up a scenario and role-play what the feedback and coaching would look like, giving your direct reports guidance on their wording or clarity. Crucially, you must remember they are the actual manager. The goal is to make them feel empowered and ensure you don't overstep their authority. I usually provide feedback on wording and will share what I understood versus what I think was intended. After a few attempts, you may need to observe their coaching session to provide focused feedback on their technique, but you should still not engage in direct coaching with the mentee. If outcomes are still not being met, I might demonstrate a coaching session directly, but always with my direct report in the room so they can see the feedback in practice, and we always debrief afterward. The goal is to create the opportunity for your managers to coach and the opportunity for you to observe.

Scale Through Stagegates

The other major shift when you become an intermediate manager is the widening of your scope, meaning you can no longer be in every meeting. The key for managing this wide scope is leading through stage gates. This is how you create agency within your team members to execute their work while defining the necessary checkpoints where you want visibility. For example, if a project has ten steps, you might say: "I'd love to see all steps one through four accomplished, check in at Step 5, continue all the way to Step 7, I want to check in at Step 8, do Step 9 on your own, and then I want to review at Step 10." Articulating your stage gates with corresponding timelines (think SMART goals) gives you the ability and confidence in your team to have agency while derisking the project. The key is to stay closely engaged at critical points.

A.4: The Department Lead

Congratulations on leading a department - it's a privilege.

Leading an Organizational Change (Reorg)

When you think about a reorg, I keep three themes top of mind: compassion, clarity, and empowerment. Being in the middle of a reorg is tough, so being compassionate when engaging with team members is mandatory. The second theme is being clear on what, why, and how things will be different. The key here is for them to feel empowered and take ownership of their choice: are they willing to upskill, and would they like the new day job? You can leverage the concepts of the Competency and Skill matrix and a Personal Development Plan to navigate options, with HR helping when needed.

Navigating the Politics

The second topic is navigating politics. When you are leading an analytics department, you will have a grounded perspective on most optics because of your access to insights. Recognize that everyone is solving for something different, which may be different than you. I focus on three ground truths to stay above the politics: first, don't lie; second, do what's right for the company and ensure the decision is defendable; and third, do what you're asked to do. The punch line is that the leadership version of "comfortable complacency" is when your assigned mandates clash with the first two principles. This may be a signal that the role is no longer a strategic fit. Things will play out with or without you, so own your transition plan.

A.5: The Executive Sponsor

One-liner: Pick someone, learn fast, and it has to work to stay the same.

Many organizations select an executive sponsor based on organizational convenience or place the burden of building or managing an Analytics, Data Science, or AI organization based on where it aligns with existing functional charters. I believe this is a suboptimal approach to capability building. The winning strategy - one that ensures the highest probability of success - is to flip the question from "Where and What?" to "Who?". We must identify the leader capable of building the capability.

I use a 2x2 matrix to organize leadership profiles that offer the highest probability of success. This framework is grounded in two critical dimensions: Organizational Stewardship (Enterprise vs. Siloed) and Execution Mindset (Operator vs. Cultivator). The four executive sponsor archetypes are defined by their organizational stewardship and execution mindset: the Visionary Transformer is an enterprise-level cultivator and the preferred archetype for driving transformation; the Scale Specialist acts as an enterprise operator but requires high investment for a lower probability of success; the Rogue Innovator is a siloed cultivator that serves as a tolerable choice only in the short term; and the Functional Expert is a siloed operator who is generally not suitable for capability building.

Bibliography

- Charan, R., Drotter, S., Noel, J. L., & Jonasen, K. (2024). The leadership pipeline: Developing leaders in the digital age (3rd ed.). John Wiley & Sons.

- Lombardo, M. M., & Barnfield, H. (2014). FYI: For Your Improvement - Competencies Development Guide (6th ed.). Minneapolis, MN: Lominger International.

- Willink, J., & Babin, L. (2015). Extreme ownership: How U.S. Navy SEALs lead and win. St. Martin's Press.

Post Credit Scene

INT. OFFICE - LATE NIGHT

MAJID sits across from a SCIENTIST, reviewing model output sheets.

SCIENTIST
(Excitedly)

Why do we need a traditional ML model when Gen AI can calculate predictions for us? See, here is an example output.

MAJID

Interesting. Have you asked the Gen AI model how it calculated that prediction?

SCIENTIST

No, the LLM calculated the prediction, of course.

MAJID

Did you ask it to confirm?

SCIENTIST

No, can I? Let me try!
(The Scientist types rapidly. After a second, a system message appears)

SYSTEM VOICE (V.O.)

I opened a Linux terminal to run Python, which used scikit-learn to build a predictive model of the sample data to generate future predictions...

MAJID
(Smiling)
See? LLMs are sequence predictors, and when the next 'word' is a command line execution, we're talking about a technology problem, not a data one. This would be an interesting book, don't you think so?